#HUMANRESOU

A SNARKY HR COLORING BOOK FOR ADULTS

DEATH BEFORE DECAF

Want free goodies?
Email us at freebies@pbleu.com

@papeteriebleu

Papeterie Bleu

Shop our other books at
www.pbleu.com

Wholesale distribution through Ingram Content Group
www.ingramcontent.com/publishers/distribution/wholesale

For questions and customer service, email us at
support@pbleu.com

FREE PDF DOWNLOAD
OF THIS BOOK

www.pbleu.com/HRLIFE

YOUR DOWNLOAD CODE: HR3773

 @papeteriebleu

 Papeterie Bleu

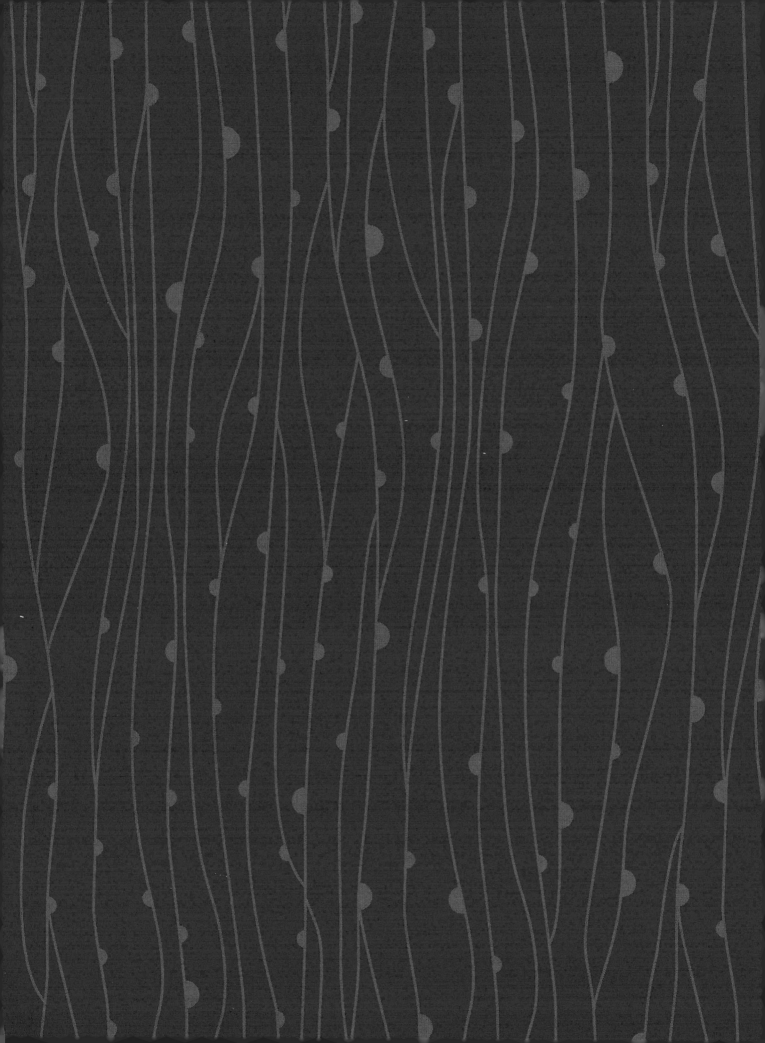

I'VE SEEN MONKEY FECES
FIGHTS AT THE ZOO
MORE
Organized
THAN MY
WORKPLACE!

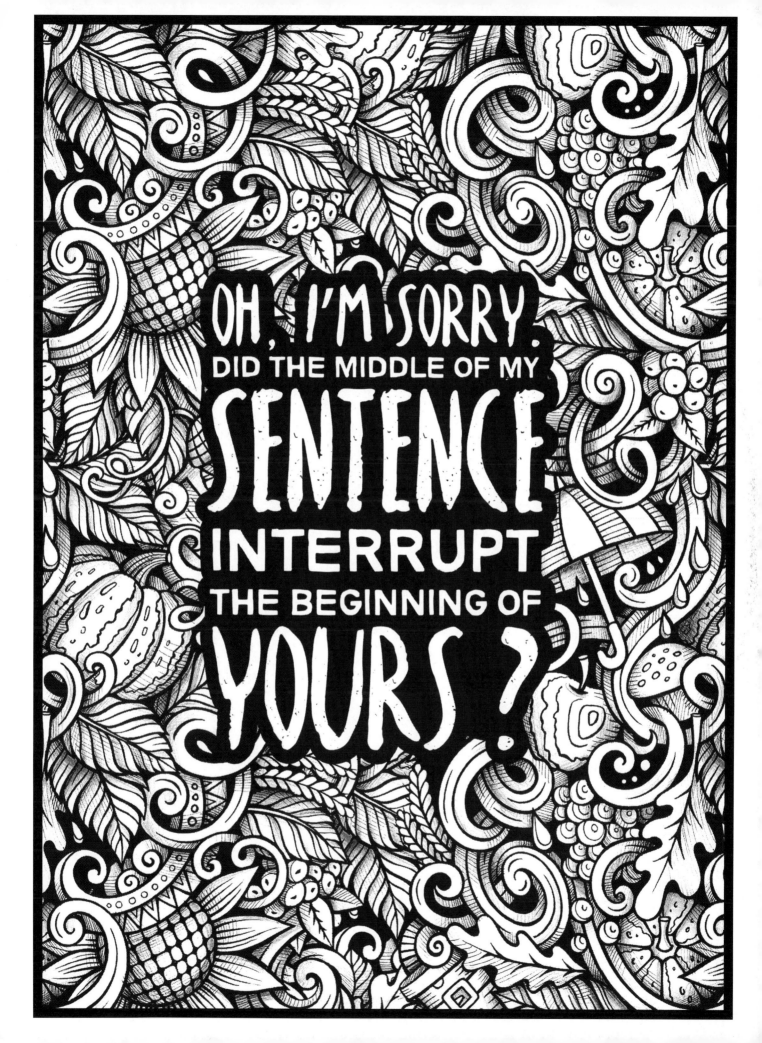

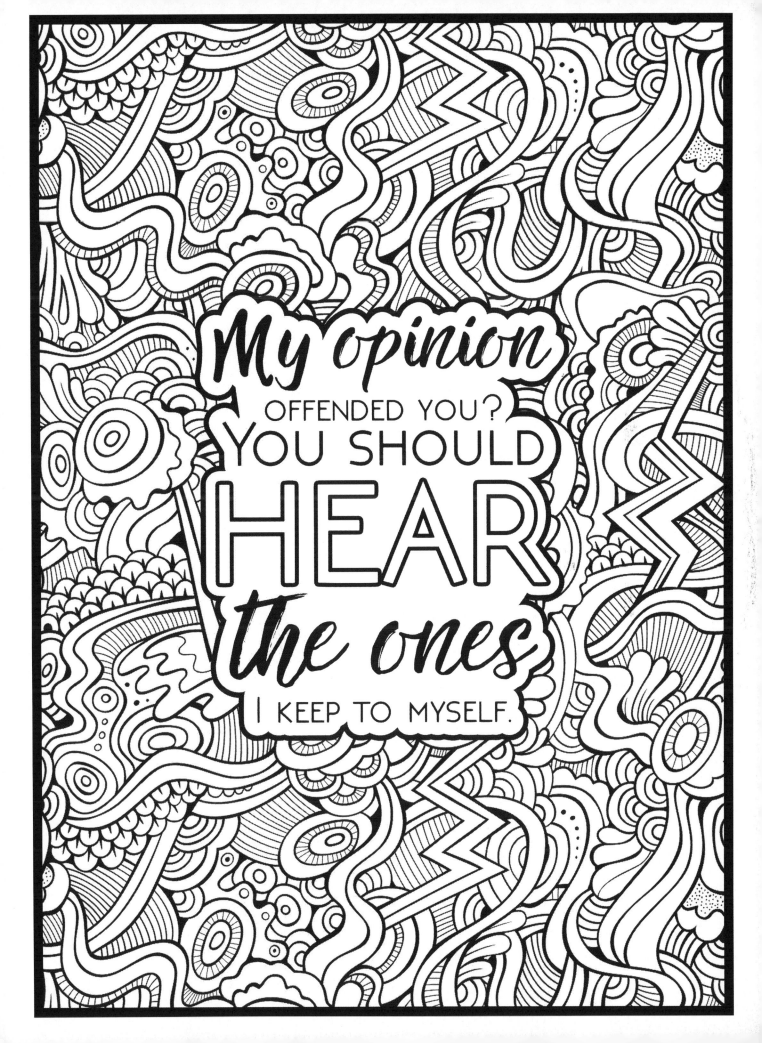

Happiness is not Having to set an alarm for TOMORROW

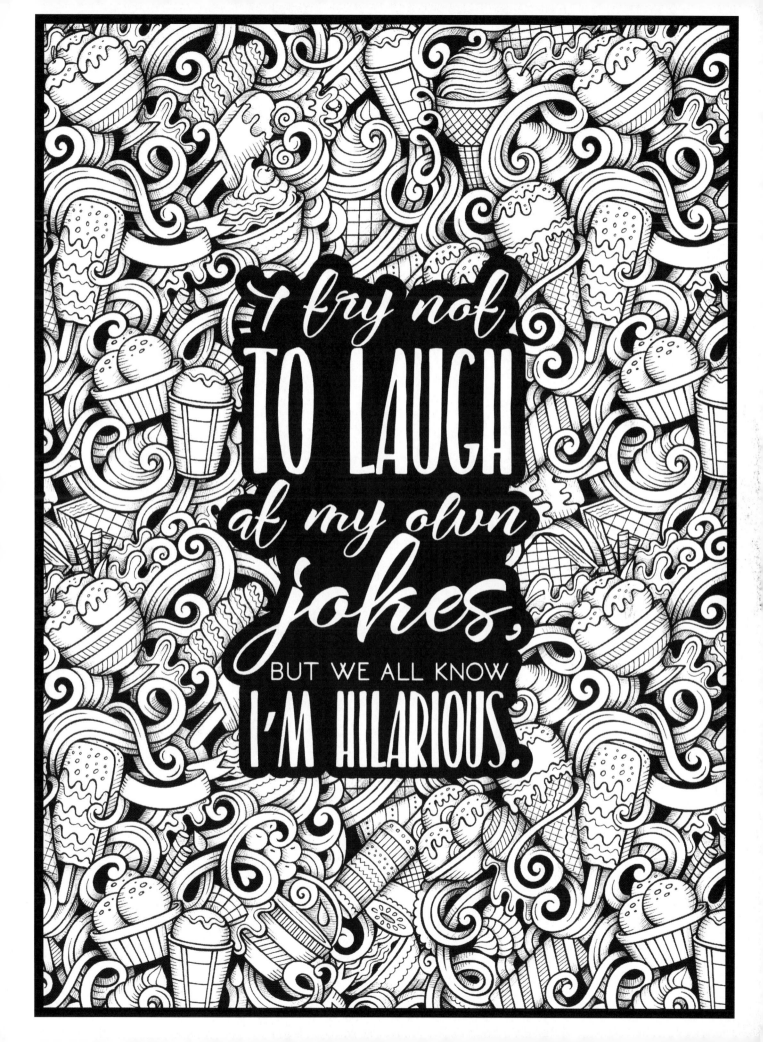

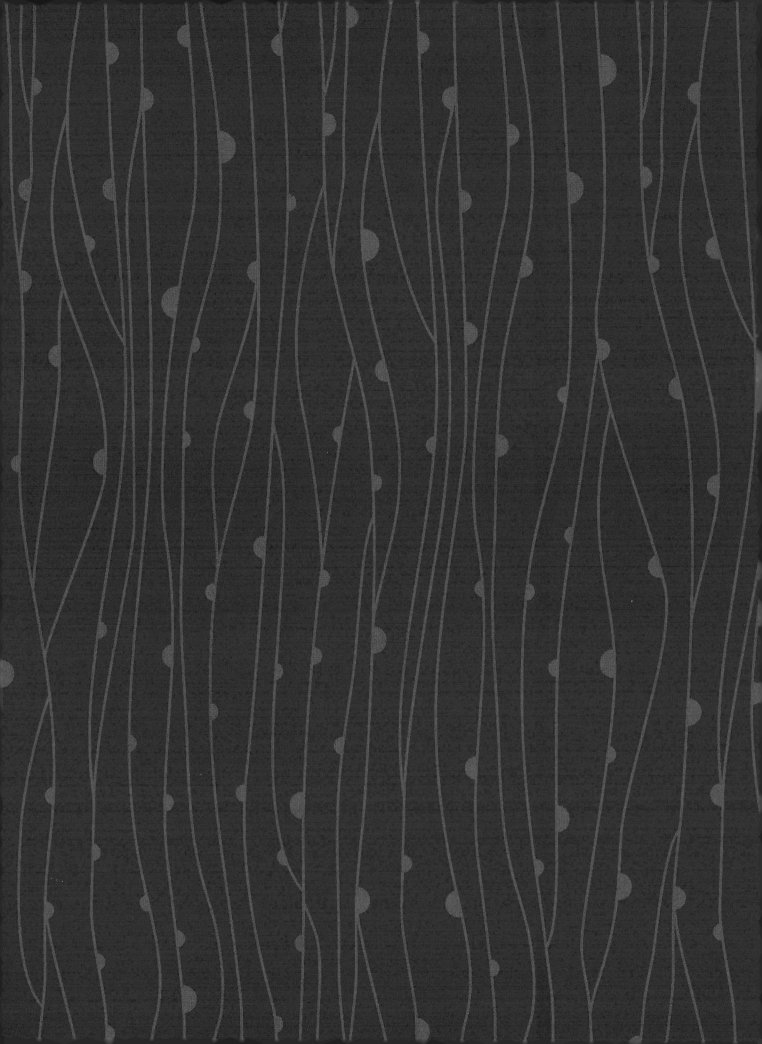

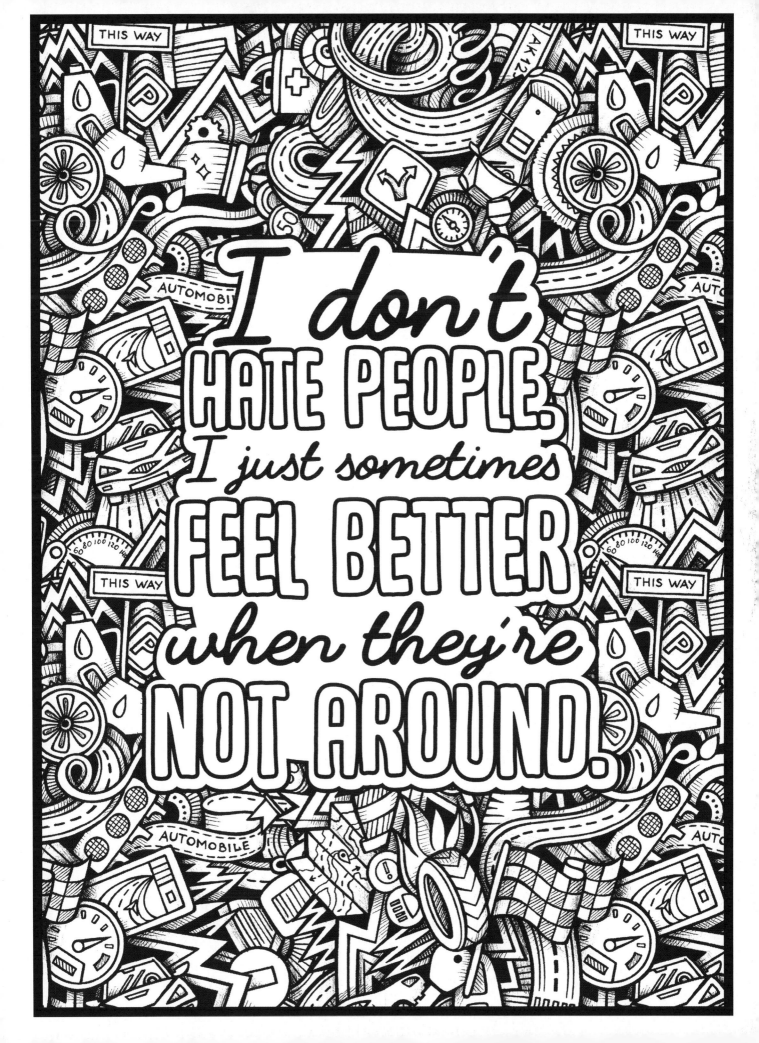

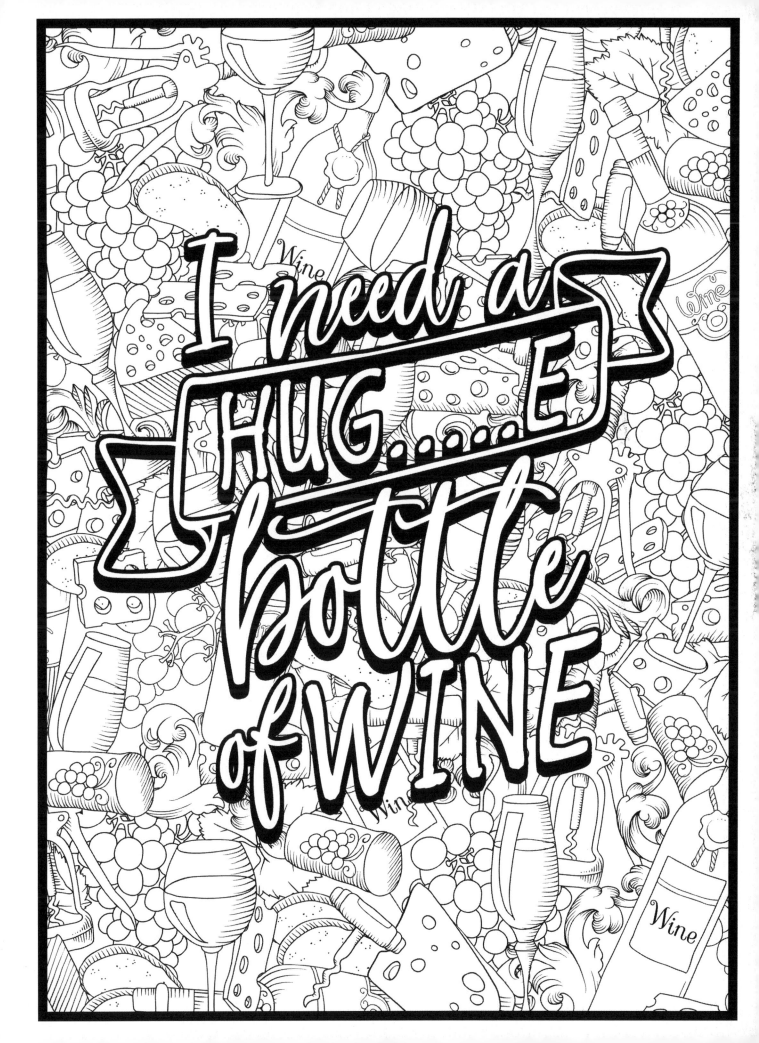

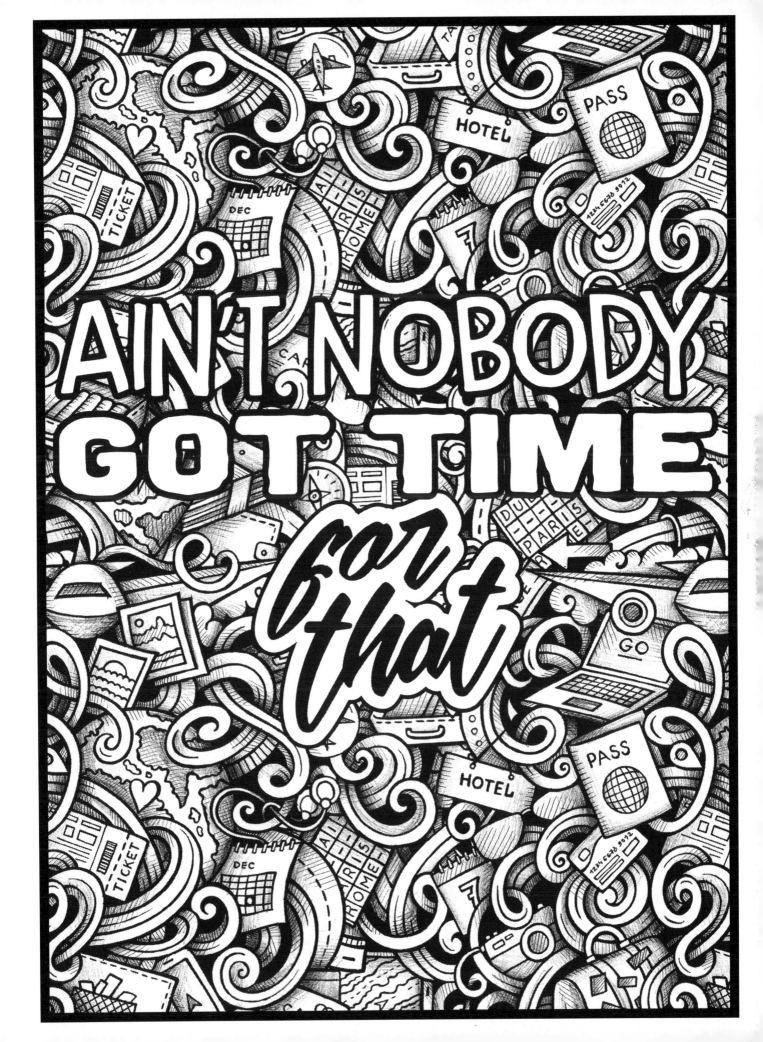

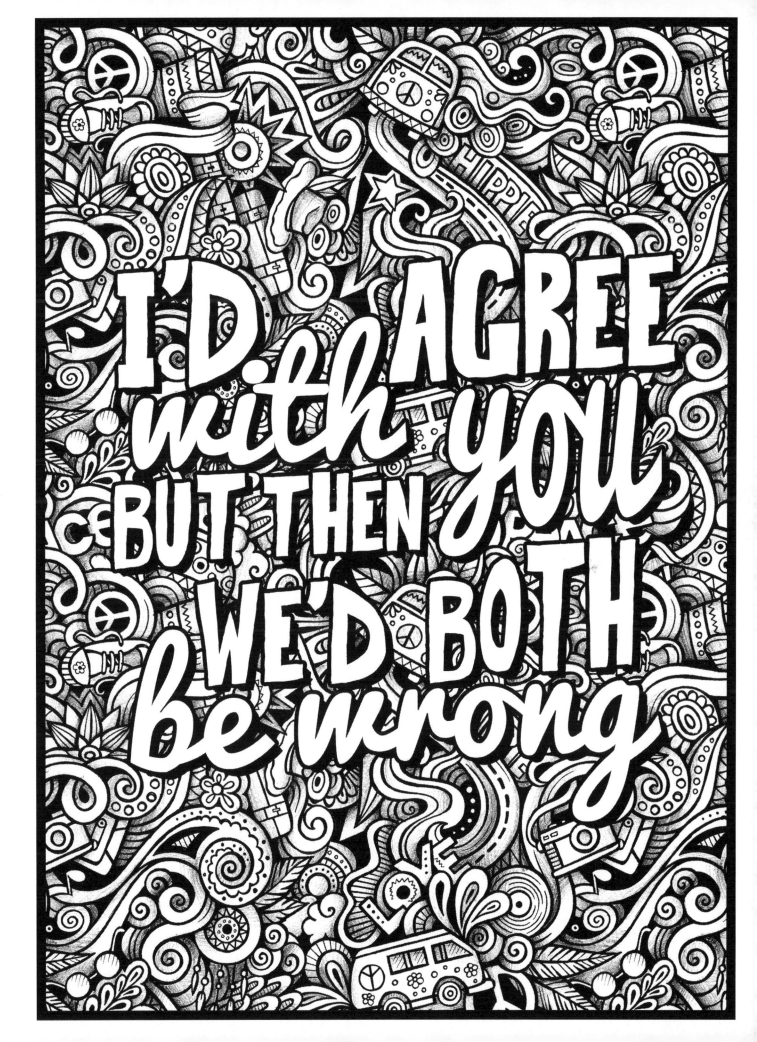

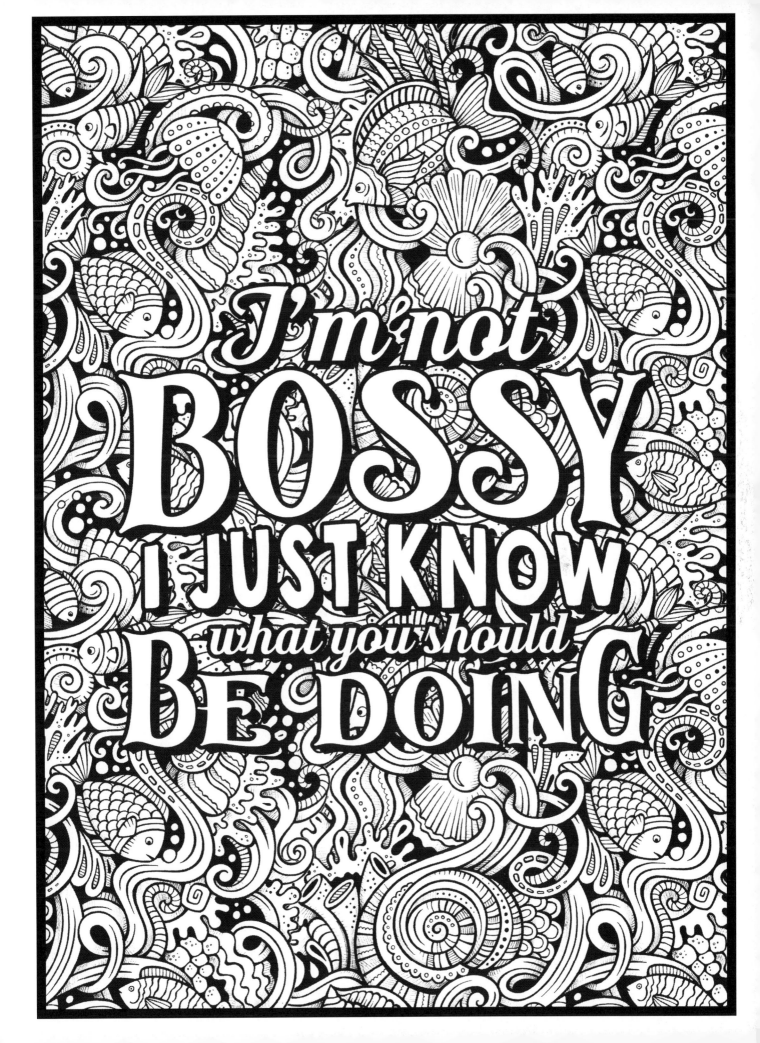

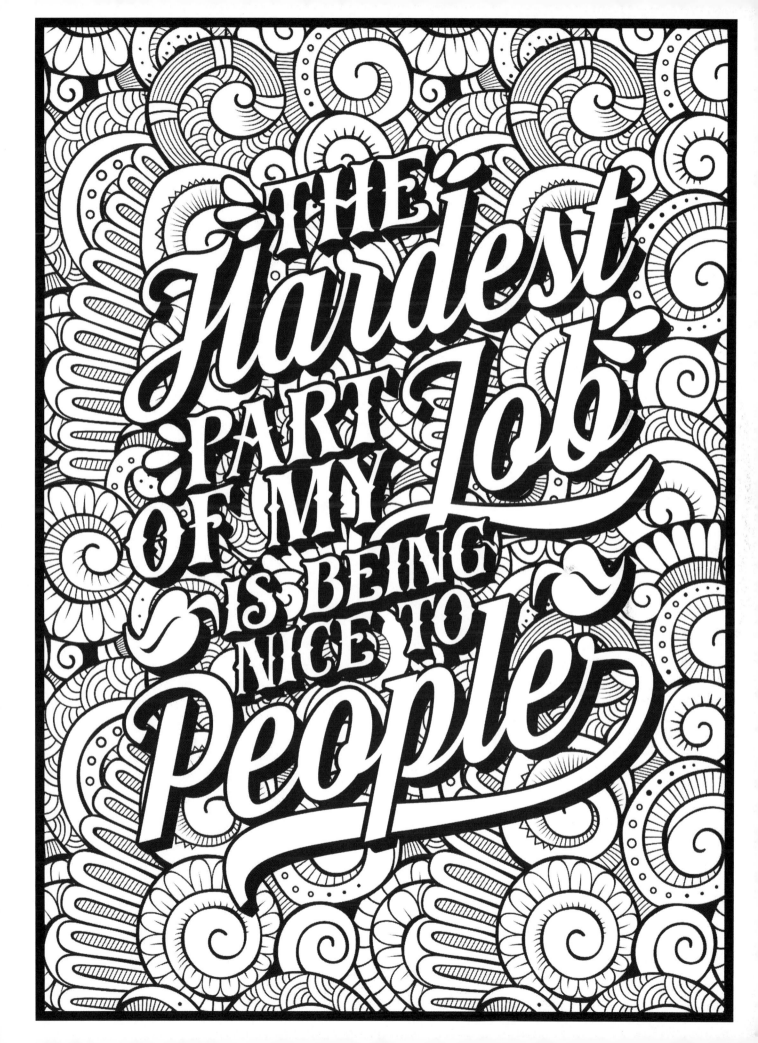

Super Cali swagilistic sexy Hella dopeness

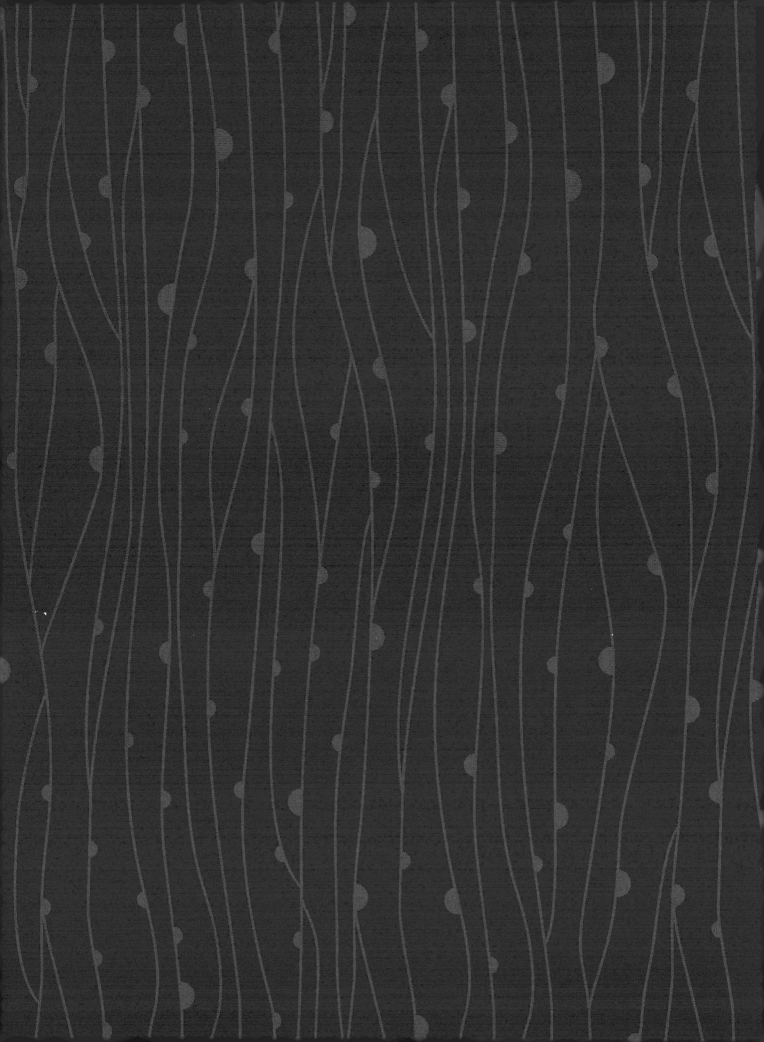

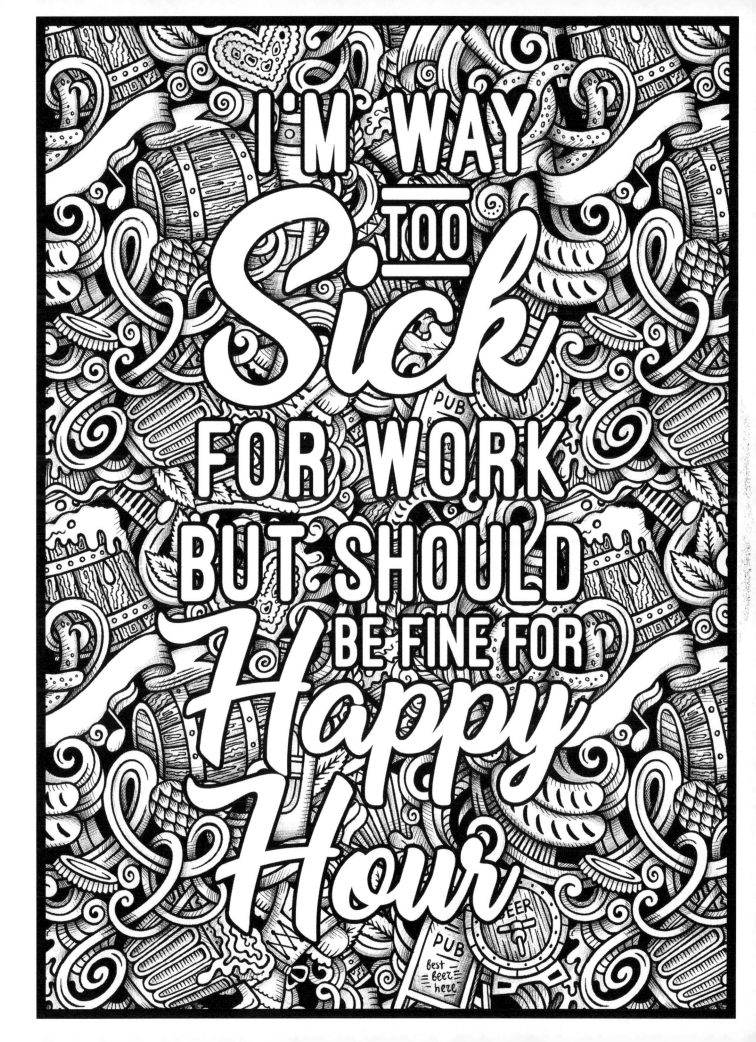

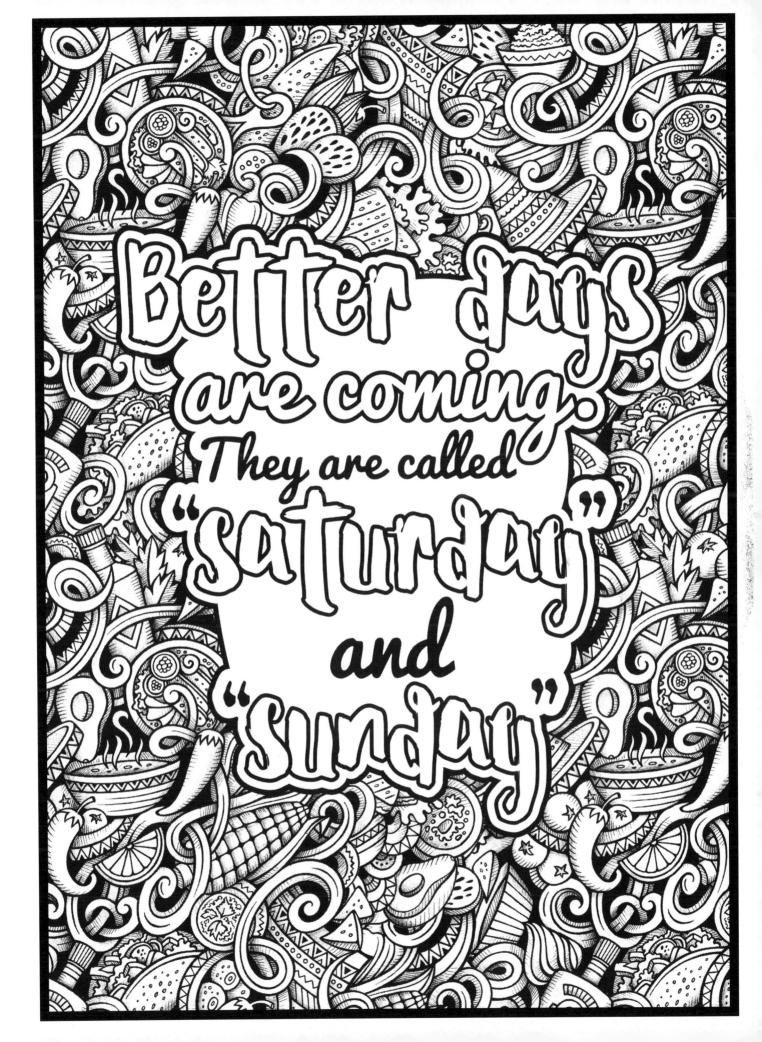

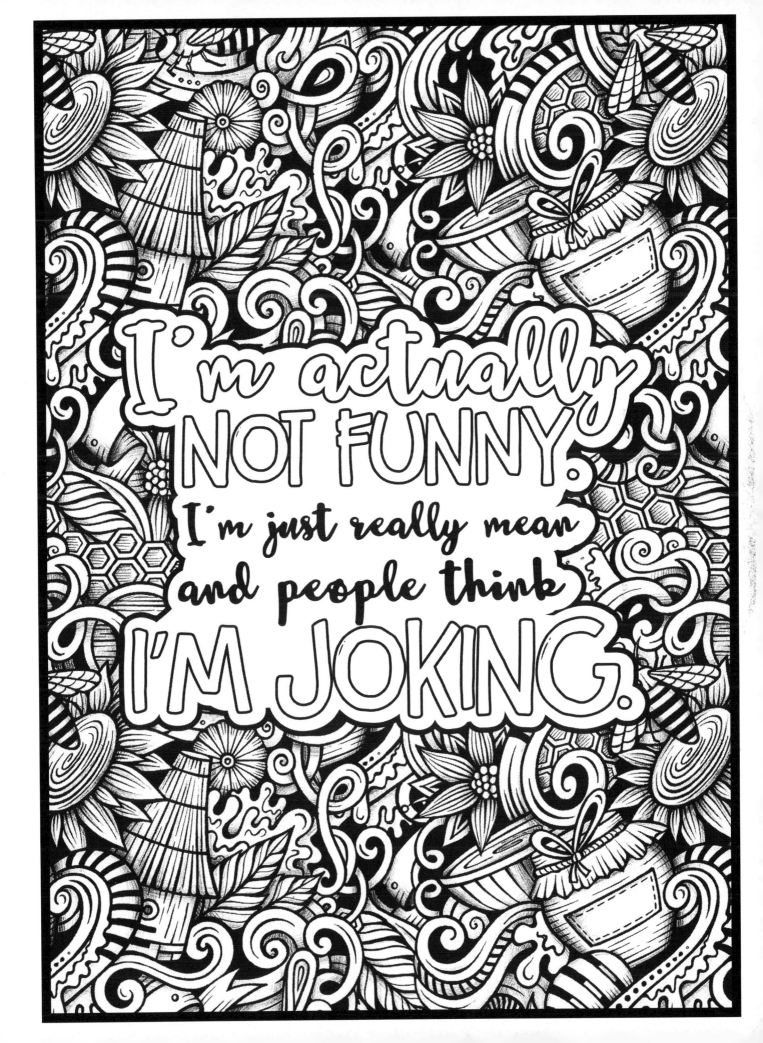

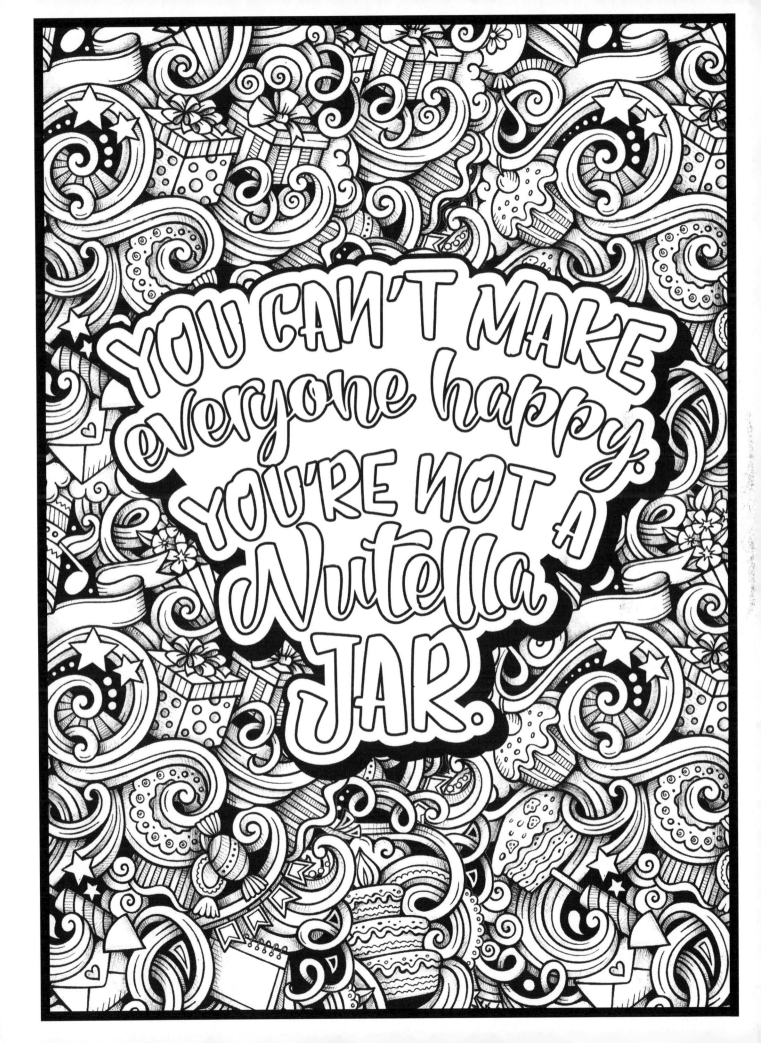

FREE PDF DOWNLOAD
OF THIS BOOK

www.pbleu.com/HRLIFE

YOUR DOWNLOAD CODE: HR3773

 @papeteriebleu

 Papeterie Bleu

Want free goodies?
Email us at freebies@pbleu.com

@papeteriebleu

Papeterie Bleu

Shop our other books at
www.pbleu.com

Wholesale distribution through Ingram Content Group
www.ingramcontent.com/publishers/distribution/wholesale

For questions and customer service, email us at
support@pbleu.com

Printed in Poland
by Amazon Fulfillment
Poland Sp. z o.o., Wrocław

53828279R00060